HORSE OF EARTH

Poems by

Thomas R. Smith

HOLY COW! PRESS

DULUTH, MINNESOTA 1994

*My heartfelt thanks to Jim Perlman for taking this Horse under his stable's
roof, and to my editor Anthony Signorelli for his unswerving attention to
both detail and essence. Gratitude as well to Perry Ingli, whose cover
painting suggests so richly the earth spirit that informs these pages. I'm also
indebted to my teachers, editors, and fellow poets for helping keep these
poems true, and to Krista, my poetry's most intimate friend.*

ISBN 0-930100-55-7

Publisher's Address: Distributor's Address:

Holy Cow! Press   The Talman Company
Post Office Box 3170   131 Spring Street
Mount Royal Station   Suite 201E-N
Duluth, Minnesota 55803   New York, New York 10012

This project is supported, in part, by a grant from the National
Endowment for the Arts in Washington, D.C., The Outagamie
Charitable Foundation, and by generous individuals.

HORSE OF EARTH

Poems by Thomas R. Smith

HORSE OF EARTH

CONTENTS

III. EATING THE COAL

IV. LIVING AS A CORMORANT

For Krista

ACKNOWLEDGMENTS

Many of these poems appeared originally, often in earlier versions, in the following publications:

The Bloomsbury Review, Calapooya Collage, The Cream City Review, Estero, Germination, The Great River Review, The Guadalupe Review, High Plains Literary Review, Inroads, The Lake Street Review, Loonfeather, Mythos Journal, North Coast Review, The North Stone Review, Raccoon, Seattle M.E.N., Sphinx (England), *Transactions of the Wisconsin Academy of Sciences, Arts and Letters, Windhorse Review, Yarrow*

Thanks to the editors of the above and of the following anthologies for permission to reprint:

"Indian Graves on Madeline Island" from *Critical Perspectives on Native American Fiction*, ed. by Richard F. Fleck, Three Continents Press

"Amish Haying Near Mt. Eaton, Ohio" from *A Song for Occupations*, ed. by Gary Schroeder and Joseph Hutchison, Wayland Press

"Cormorant" and "Listening to Robert Bly at Unity Church" from *Walking Swiftly: Writings and Images on the Occasion of Robert Bly's 65th Birthday*, ed. by Thomas R. Smith, Ally Press

"Thistledown" from *Wisconsin Poetry*, ed. by Bruce Taylor, Wisconsin Academy of Sciences, Arts and Letters

"Rejoicing Over Death" and "Contempt" from *Rooster Crows at Light from the Bombing*, ed. by Paul MacAdam and Anthony Signorelli, Inroads Press

*Don't be the rider who gallops all night
and never sees the horse that is beneath him.*

Rumi

LETTING THE HORSE OUT OF MY HOUSE

I knew the time was right by the way sunlight over-
brimmed the inrolling surf and climbed the gentle slope
to illuminate my house of white and salt-flecked maple.
I knew the horse was ready by its tautness when

I reached to stroke its firm, substantial neck:
Inside I could hear blood barely contained,
hooves pounding from the age of tiny ancestors.
And silently the horse with pale gold mane

let me pilot its heavy boat along the narrow
hallway, down the backstairs, and under a low doorsill,
tight channel not chafing the bowed ribs, to stand
whole and suddenly alone, breathing the bright air of the sea.

I.

DAYS TOGETHER

For love has to be so,
involving and general,
particular and terrifying,
honored and yet in mourning,
flowering like the stars,
and measureless as a kiss.

Pablo Neruda

GATE WREATHED WITH ROSES

The summer door flew open,
light and breathless music tumbled out.
Your hair shivered gold, your dress
whirled, and I knew from the dance

we would soon be lovers. And what if
we'd danced and left it at that,
come so far in the woods toward
each other from separate births

and not chosen? I could have
kept you, another sad picture,
in one of those bottles
from which I drank my own failure.

But something stronger than myself
chose, was not about to lose,
and chose more decisively than
we could have. Say it was

an angel waiting in us with its sword
of daylight raised against a burning
darkness. It showed me your gate
wreathed with roses before my life's

perishing garden, and I went in—
although that was a different man,
unsure of his courage, who bargained with the angel
and agreed to die to enter that garden.

SPLITTING WOOD

Beginning, a stroke may swing far
from true, axe handle ring offended
on the log, the blade cleave dirt.
A near-miss may shear off kindling strips,
of use but not what we wanted.
Measured by eye, then commended to muscle,
nerve and old inner knowledge of sundering,
a direct hit down the middle halves so decisively
we wonder if this was the way
a Platonic creator struck from us our soul's
own missing part for whom we secretly long
during the afternoons of wood-splitting,
the nights of wood-burning. We feel
in palms and chest the driving line
of the blade's edge making contact,
and the lightning shock along the grain's
utter distance. A single gesture prepared
in the lift of arches uncoils in knees
and the hollow of the back, arcs from
wrist-bone to shaft-wood, and shudders earthward
between the one now two falling each
from itself, its faces white
with disjoining, each having become a face
only now, separated from another.

OLIVET

Saying yes to you in my heart, I took
the long way home at sunset,
pulled off the road at a junction called Olivet.
On clotheslines I saw the sad sheets

of the married, of the desire
not to travel on alone.
A house of dust, its beams on fire,
gathered itself around me.

A one-room school overgrown with burdock,
its broken windows brushed by the red wing
of the west, stood apart from the white houses
as I, for years, had stood apart.

The dirt road loves the fields as they are.
That was the kind of love you gave me.
There are places I have driven by only once
and lived in the rest of my life.

THE STRAWBERRIES

One summer evening
the year we found each other
in the dark of Wisconsin,
we sat on your porch drinking
glasses of chilled white wine.
How quickly the August heat
stole into them as we
fingered perspiring stems!
Afterward I'd walked nearly
two blocks from the amber-
lit steps of that house where
next autumn we'd both live,
when I heard you behind me
as if called by my longing
for you, running breathlessly
to press in my palm strawberries
still cold from your icebox.

Now the simple days and nights
when we stood revealed
in each other's light
for the first time
are gone, gone as the sleepless
affection of those weeks.
I will not mourn them—
they were seeds that entered
earth to make a place
for our desire to grow.
You brought those first fruits

of a summer's plenty
to my open palm, and
blossoms that gave brief glories
to the bedsides of our loving.

The harvests already taken
are alive in the new harvest.
And the strawberries
of that summer night so long ago,
whose red pulp passed from chill
to warm on my tongue and then,
in new-found boldness given
with a kiss, on yours,
shine in us still,
red constellation by which
we reckon our position,
begin again to lose our fear
and find once more original courage
that brought us near in the beginning.

GRATITUDE

A gratitude I could not speak became tears.
It was the gratitude of the maple leaf
wedded to the October sky,
the gold the reeds give back
to the darkness that sent them.
And the gold of the reeds was in your hair
and in the late sun on your face, neither
young nor old then, the face of a wife.

Clouds of roe swirl in chill
northern waters, and so few live!
Acorns rattle down in autumn gusts,
a whole forest from a single oak tree,
yet few strike roots of their own.
It must be we are chosen for life or death
by a love greater than either, felt by a man
and woman rowing in the middle of the lake.

Neighboring lakes have commerce beneath fields.
The water of the higher one wells up
from hillsides among the horsetails,
streams filtered through rock and sand
reach down to touch the lake below.

BRIDE'S MOON

Reed beds stretch out like a tawny animal on the water.
Pale rose petals band slowly across the lake at dusk.
The woman newly married twines red willow withies for her basket.
The rising moon knows the white fish feeding near shore.

DAYS TOGETHER

In October, I walk over the mapled ridge.
The lake's dazzle spreads among bare trees,
heads of pampas grass catch the tarnished
silver.... These are the clear days,
days of a few words—a poem, a promise,
a welcome—burning against the sky.

In autumn our thoughts become as simple
and complex as the hairs on a staghorn sumac.
Our days bring us more and more to this world,
looking at what is before our eyes,
hearing sounds, and feeling beneath us
the horse of earth on which we ride.

IN A CANOE ON CLEARWATER LAKE

Each stroke of the paddle raises the coolness of autumn.
Reeds brush the sides and bottom of the canoe—
even those stiff and brown with age bend as we pass.

You and I, married only these few days, float
above so much we do not see! Our small craft
drifts negligently when we do not stir the water.

THE BLOSSOM

When we love, clouds
of early spring fly over,
neither snow nor rain.
A joy whose name
waits to be spoken
hides in the new moon.
At the edge of the bed,
you tighten your legs
on my waist. How many
centuries have we
done this thing?
What was sleeping
between our thighs hears
the flute sound
that persuaded the tulip
to throw open the bulb's
bronze door. Our most
sheltered bud,
when it meets another,
falls into a wild desire
to unfold itself and
become a blossom—
all children, reckless,
ride into this world
on the promise
of that burning blossom.

LEGEND

My German grandparents lived their lives
in a room they called 'Christ.'
In my dream I opened the door,
saw the dotted Swiss curtains stir
as early morning breeze and birdsong
through a raised window woke them.

It is a day in summer, in the midstream
of their lives. They hear voices
in the house, grown daughters
already up and brewing coffee.
Soon they'll rise and secretly kiss
before donning the dark cloth of custom.

My grandfather will walk among the bridal veil
still fresh with dew, a measured
briskness in his stride, brooding
on next Sunday's sermon. My grandmother
will kneel in her garden, in fat brown loam
that pales quickly in the intense June heat.

And the bed, freshly made with its quilt
of Old World roses, broken gateway for thirteen
souls, will become again a hopeful thing,
its channel widening to a river,
rich in possibility as a young girl,
or a legend, or a potato field in blossom.

ANNIVERSARY POEM

Fallen juniper berries
bring a second summer,
as if chicory and asters
have returned to meadows.
They are blue stars
still cloudy with creation,
as the first man and woman
must have seen them.
By those stars we two set out.

The boat leaving the harbor
seems hesitant
to let the wind move it.
The fabric ripples, then
goes slack. Years pass,
driving each life toward
the emptiness of the acorn cap
on its branch in October,
the fringed cup downed
and filled again with memory
and triumph.
                    After two years,
I touch you, still amazed.
Our small boat follows
the water's curved ache,
a strong breeze billowing its sails.

A BLESSING

Ten yellow tulips streaked with red
stand in a vase in morning sunlight.
It is Sunday, you are gone to church,
and I am at the desk, moving fragments
of a broken kingdom. Like Ponge,
I would take the world piece by piece,
"as it comes to me," into the workshop
for repairs, knowing the mechanic also
is damaged, in need of repair.

Yet last night together we drank
from some whole and original flower
in the gold shadow of our loving.
You said, "The body grows out of
the spirit," and for a moment I saw
how the honey attracts the honeycomb,
how the bee's black jaws and forelegs
molding the wax are our willingness
to write down dreams.

Ten tulips stand in Sunday
morning triumph, flames rising
from the oil lamps of joy. They
journey together and alone, and bring
from below a gift that might
have remained locked in corpses,
earth and night but for a
blessing, each now a chamber
in air for some risen devotion.

A READINESS TO WEEP

Five years later, we have returned
to the lake where we spent our
honeymoon, two people who knew
even less about marriage than we do.
I had refused for years, then
gave in because I feared some damage
to your happiness with me.
"I did it," I told you,
"but I don't know what it means,"

and wept. Today, a day clear
as that one we drove down the dirt
road to the cabin after the wedding,
I squat in these marshy woods
that have remained, in my mind, October
and give again my gift from
five years ago, a readiness to weep.

I sit quietly in the sunlight
with you and feel the years, and
do not feel them. I let the peach-flushed
leaf I saved fall from my hand—
Yes, I want time to stop for us,
doesn't everyone?—No, I let it go.

The fallen branch we sat on breaks
suddenly but lets us down unharmed—
the ground isn't in the least sentimental.
We laugh together, then the tears again.

I soak my knees, leaning to cup
in hands chill water from the lake
to splash over my burning eyes.

When I look up,
every man and woman ever married
look with me across the autumn lake
toward the gold pavilions of uncertainty.

II.

WINDFALL APPLES

LOON'S FLIGHT
For Melanie Richards

The loon glides above the lake at sunset,
sharp wings creasing the overbrimming light.
Hers is a life lived best offshore,
of perfect landings and difficult departures.
Riding low among waves, she wallops
her watery runway taking flight, her voice
pitched to the quavery frequencies of adolescence,
a beginner every time. Aloft, she steadies,
her black neck tapering after an airy quick
never to be possessed, touched only by what changes,
found again in each ungainly ascent.

MARCH WIND

Across the channel of the Minnesota River,
a long shiver passes through the body of a pine grove.
Scaly ice shelves up along the waterline,
the walker beside it easily lost in the great silent day of spring.

I walk with you on a sandy path on the island.
In the maple trunks a slender sweetness rises and falls.
The nights are still cold. Maple sap boils dark and heavy.
I catch the clear drops, almost flavorless, on a torn branch in
    the wind.

THE SNAKESKIN

Morning smells of rain and wet hay banked against the foundation of the house from last winter. The snakeskin stretches on grass near the porch, damp, about four feet long, a breath exhaled by a dream just before it disappeared at sunrise. Someone has outworn a former life here, abandoned a perfected style to reinhabit the vulnerable, luminous and raw.

A pattern emerges as the skin dries, thousands of fingertip-sized markings, the dark of old photographic negatives. Each scale suggests a miniature landscape drawn with a single hair from a sumi brush. The portholes of the eyes give out onto an ocean of dew the snake's belly navigates. Below the eyes, a mouth with open jaws, the skin curled back to form fleshless lips whispering that Pythagoras was right....

The tail's rows of hexagonal boxes diminish toward the invisible. These six-sided houses empty one after another into the place where lovers go when they are done with owning things, where there is no difference between their love and the sound of wind in winter oak leaves....

THE BREASTS

I lie with my hand pressed
between your breasts' divided fall,
the flat of my thumb on your rippled breastbone,
and remember that mild November afternoon
we climbed the bluff at Rocky Branch.
In the late, unasked-for
warmth, we stripped to our waists
and basked above the shadows slowly pooling
the autumn dusk in the coulees.
You were in your late twenties, chest
nearly shallow as my own. The nipples'
brown roses opened thirstily to my touch
as if the loneliness in my body were enough
to call your womanhood budding outward
to meet me. Thus a slender girl in you
followed love into her fullness, while I,
who had hovered above my body for years,
fell into the blood and bones of a man.
Sometimes in dreams or in a mirror,
I'll glimpse that lost boy, hear his voice
of glass, in moments of panic feel his thinness.
And you, who breathe so calmly beside me,
as if you were always and only this one
clasping in her doubled embrace of woman's
tenderest flesh my hand grown familiar
from thousands of nights—Is there still
in your dreaming a girl who waits uncertainly
for springtime at the edge of an unblossoming field?

THE WILD ROSES

1.

In poor cemeteries you sometimes
see only a metal rod supporting a vase
or a square of white marble sunk
like a mooring block at high tide....
The grass of May was wet and green.
Small flowers, a papier-mâché urn
tipped over, melting in the rain.
Someone's large hand led me away.

2.

Walking in a cemetery above a town
where I am a stranger, I think
of them again, those four stillborn sisters
poured back in the earth like green wine,
and wonder if even my mother can still
find their four unmarked graves.
A papier-mâché urn fallen in spring rain...

3.

Wild roses search the fenceline, watery stars
rayed with pink among the dark leaves.
Where does the soul of a rose go when it dies?
Under the Norway pines I kneel and count
the five rayed petals of the pasture roses:
four for the four who fluttered toward the light
and one for the one in me who keeps their darkness.

A PRIVATE GRIEF

In woods where I've walked all morning,
meeting no one, the long grass lies down
elegant and rank. Why does it sadden me,
as if my life were a countryside never visited?

Bunches of needles fall from white pines
and smolder like matchsticks
on the grass. They are the gift
we were given, but learned of too late.

We are a flash of feathers among bushes,
a turning in the path, a crow's harsh cry
above the trees. In an afternoon our silhouette
can be washed away by September rain.

A song we have loved for centuries goes away.
Our line entwines with the one growing faint.

INDIAN GRAVES ON MADELINE ISLAND
For Gerald Vizenor

It startles us to come upon this tract, despite our having known of it, beyond the shops of La Pointe. Labor Day, the last wave of tourism before mist and finally ice enclose the island. Masts of yachts weave above the broken pickets and uncut grass, the dusty trees and boulders. Dirt paths are worn between graves marked with either an illegible wafer of white marble or a weathered grave house. A cross of twigs lashed with yellow grass leans against each marker.

Gulls flail in wind, and know nothing of the scarcities we invent for ourselves, for others. Their cries make us eager to live, to outlive those who died within view of the red cliffs of the mainland. Linda Cadotte, at 40, laid her name here among her people's names in 1981. Lines by Edna St. Vincent Millay on her solitary modern stone rebuke the tall money of the marina:

SAFE UPON THE SOLID ROCK THE
UGLY HOUSES STAND
COME AND SEE MY SHINING PALACE
BUILT UPON THE SAND

Come and see the beautiful shacks in the weeds, doors and windows sunken, thrown open to the other world. Wood shingles stumble downward with finality, a story ending in betrayal and drunkenness, in the teller weeping. These houses aren't for staying, but are roads Ojibway souls follow for four days, nourished on wild rice, maple sugar and the wishes of the living, leaving behind in concealed drawers in the plain pine board structures only shadows and silence....

THE WINTER APPLE

In memory of Judith Rathke,
whose birthday and mine are the same

In January old nests stand empty.
The singing bird is elsewhere.
What is left of childhood and summer
but a few black leaves curled in grass,
the powdered face in the coffin, buildings
so plain on the small town main street in winter....

My Aunt Judy, eldest of the living Rathke
women, wept for me when I left for Europe,
twenty-nine years old, with a thousand
dollars in my pocket and no return ticket.
A stout woman who wore dark dresses to a
shine, her hands smelled of coffee and prayer.

Judy alone of my mother's sisters never
married. Her heavy breasts belonged
to someone we can't see clearly anymore—
the God of her father, or years when
"no man was good enough," a woman
who roomed with her, or perhaps both.

Without children of her own, my aunt made
of her thick-ankled body a firm house
for our affection, gave from her ampleness
a nectar, as the winter apple alone
on a branch neglected by the pruner
opens and shrivels to wholly core.

There is a snowfall inside some old women
that leaves them silent, their windows dark.
Finally the nephew sends no more cards,
throws the shredded rag rug in the trash.
Mortal fibers part, but not the links
the heart made plaiting its wish.

AMISH HAYING NEAR MT. EATON, OHIO

Two boys and a girl rode a golden cloud
across the swelling rows of a hayfield.
The smaller boy drove the team:
Planted dark and peg-like at the reins,
he was already man at ten or twelve years.
By hand, the girl arranged deftly the hay
forked forward by the taller boy—
gold glittered in the strands sweated loose
from the law tight about her forehead.
With that titanism of young hayers,
the boy with the fork stood balanced,
pitched load after load past his shoulders
as mechanical rakes gripped the green-
gold piles and raised them from stubble.
All three waved to us from their labor
as the wagon reached row's end
and pivoted back along the way it had come.
How silent they seemed and buoyant despite
their effort, breeze lifting errant hay
and hair in the Ohio sun,
pulled in their swaying ark of weathered planks,
the only sounds the creaking of harnesses,
horses' plodding, the brush and crackle
of unbound hay, the slender rattling of rakes.

PALMINA

I have seen her strong face elsewhere,
her face worked intricately by time
like the lace of Brugge and useful
as a loaf of bread or a boot,
her stout legs planted in the dust
like sycamores, and her eyes that weigh
and balance like a farmer at market.

This robust woman of Maastricht
bore her first child by lantern light
while Allied planes and mortars smashed
the line held for five years by the Nazis.
Half a century later in Beja, Portugal,
her lean husband raises his cup: "We still
remember how you Americans liberated us."

Palmina brings us hearty Dutch stew
flavored with yellow broccoli flowers
to eat in our tent, and red
wine to drink in the Alentejo sun,
and when we try to thank her exclaims
as she always does, "No thanks at all!"

We accept the cup of years
she has offered, and agree to taste
their darkness and strength: For the gift
of age is to pass the cup full,
youth's gift to hand it back emptied.

ANTONIO MACHADO'S MARRIAGE

The young soldier and his girlfriend
leave the cheap pension at dawn.
They stop to admire shoes in a shop
window, then vanish into the subway
entrance at Puerta del Sol. And no one
knows yet what the clay of Extremadura
keeps to give back on the last day.

In a depleted mountain town along the Duero,
a man and woman stand arm in arm
before the photographer's backdrop, a turn-
of-the-century garden. In their untrustworthy
paradise, the schoolteacher poet, unsmiling,
seems protective of the dark-haired bride
who will not live past seventeen. He will
later write, "She is with me always."

How many dusty plazas in early afternoon
are encased in the word 'always':
Nights to drink from the philosophers
a guarded optimism, and write
by the ticking of a clock of vowels
sad and hopeful lines addressed
to the memory of an almond-like flowering
whose moment he called Leonor:
Narrow highway between tedium and dreams.

Once in November on the road to Madrid,
an old woman outside a tavern plucked
yellow windfall apples from deep grass
and bundled them in her shawl.
Later, on the bus, her husband
sliced carefully in quarters with a pocketknife
that fruit which the night frosts of Castile
had struck through with a watery sweetness.

In Soria golden leaves of poplars
quiver on foothills of the Guadarrama.
Something entering earth has promised to return,
as on the day the photographer
threw the black cloth over his head:
Leonor's hand rests lightly as a canary
on the dark sleeve destined to slant
a mournful ray over pages of her absence,
difficult faith that the poem can be that earth
which remembers the moist glow inside
each apple she will not have him cut for her.

THISTLEDOWN

After long heat, the sun floats pale
above the oak savanna, its edges drawn.
Now begins the movement inward,
withdrawing its flame from the high places
of summer and striving, to fully inhabit
its depths, its ring of steady warmth.

For it is the warmth, not the fire,
of long-lasting love which endures the burning-
off of years and bodies, stirred in us now
by that autumnal heartbeat. Two crows
fly together, their cries going out before them
to meet the darkening burr oaks on the hill.

Thistledown falls as if from open drawers, fold
upon fold of linens tumbled before the goldenrod.
On its own journey, the sower of thistles
travels with us, a homespun beauty finely feathered.
I lift one to the wind, coppery wings carry it
over fields toward the inward-circling sun.

III.

EATING THE COAL

EATING THE COAL

Spain, 1986
On the 50th anniversary of Federico García Lorca's murder

We cannot remain only where we love.
We must enter the neglected places
where care has been neither given
nor taken. We must go down
in the mine and eat the coal.

Traveling that winter in a country not my own,
I dreamt of men who loved the good dark
kneeling around a hole in the basement floor.
Alone, each man climbed down a ladder,
disappeared, and returned.
I saw the streaked brow and
forearm of a man I felt close to
who offered me a sacrament if I would
go down in the mine and eat the coal.

In the dream, I weighed the chunk
in hand before biting in.
Bitter taste of cinders, failure,
black honeycomb of generations'
striving and falling back
between the black, beaten leaves of earth:
then the honey, a sun rising,
boys running in springtime,
old buildings settled on stone foundations...

In America, soft monsters expire daily.
Bare windows rattle, a thunder
of dissolution rips the industrial plain.
Shouting men push a broken-down Lincoln
on a freeway where nothing is free
but an unattached darkness sifting down.

But I woke from my dream in a country
still crossed by the sun and moon
and by their four kinds of shadow,
where one morning before sunrise
Lorca went down with his poems
in the mine between two olive trees
and became the coal.

COME IN FROM THE RAIN!

Many remain mute. This one kneels
on a folded blanket sodden with rain
and sways toward the wall, his face
floating in the long bay of his hands.

He is one of the sad beggars of Barcelona
who kneel on sidewalks barefoot, hold out
cigar boxes, display some deformity or wound.
Some grip signs saying merely, "I am hungry."

Coins dropped on his laboriously printed plea
glisten, kings' faces drowning. He seems
oblivious of the winter wind in the alley,
the great stains devouring his shoes.

Such men turn up without explanation
or history on the streets of every city
of the world, delivered in our path
as if ejected by some shabby womb

to be rained on or frozen drunk
under a viaduct, without dry clothes
or honor. *For God's sake, man,*
it's time to come in from the rain!

But I do not say it. Beneath my
umbrella, I'm unsure whether I'm addressing
this Gypsy—master of a cruel discipline—
or my father, my brother, men of my country.

CATTAILS

I love the desolation of this lake shore in April,
a loneliness not desperate for relief—
the way the moist sand seems to accept for now
the free and careless litter of sticks and reeds.

And last year's cattails stand bleached
and brittle: only the stalks remain,
the loaves of reddish seed now furred away.
What have men together without grief?

The cattail seed loses its brotherhood,
goes down in the mud to die alone.
Men grieve together, and sometimes in spring
a man stands up green and tall from the lake of tears.

THE SOPRANO

The conductor brings up violins behind the heavy-breasted woman. Tonight she is singing *Four Last Songs* by Strauss. Her knees bend, she lists to one side like a boat on the Rhine.

Notes stream upward, almost inaudible, the stirring of a breeze among oak leaves or the sounds river ice makes in early spring. Suddenly what was listened for so carefully is loose in air, a passion declared after years of concealment, a storm arriving on a clear day. In a valley, sunlight flees the ripened clusters of grapes. So many not tasted, paintings never seen, cities that waited for us and we did not come...

The audience feels fear beneath the intoxicating melody. In the voice's distillation is a summing up, a precise accounting of its existence, a rose fully opened in this room. The hearer glimpses not only the strength and subtlety of the soul, but its dark seams also, niches of character, dislocations and failings. How difficult it is to be a woman, the grief of the new life turning in her earthen body. And then—how difficult it is to be human. The man is inside the woman and the woman inside the man, and they have never met.

THE DEMOLISHED ANTHILL
For Allan Cooper

A disaster has burst the sod and turf container of this ant town under the low-hanging shed of pines. Probably the anthill owes its devastation to a black bear foraging these Fundy woods in springtime, ripping up its living commons by the pawful.

The dome, coarse and bulging, caves slowly forward to an empty face, the eyes and nose clawed away by some savagery in the economic system. The ruin is framed by a mat of tasseled grey grass resembling wheat or hops, the beard of Dionysus in dismemberment.

It is difficult to imagine any regeneration for this exploded mound after the further attrition of rain. The few citizens still occupying its wounded labyrinth live in seclusion, although now and then one motors over a pine-needle-choked dirt road, a ninety-year-old man driving his pickup truck despite near-blindness....

Alma, New Brunswick, May 1989

A MASCULINE LONGING

In a cream-colored room with blue curtains,
a woman in long skirts gazes at her lamp.
She perfects the art of longing. In poems I have
gone with her to that room, escaped with relief
the travail of the fathers, their difficult
beauty, made no room in my words for the wood
they chopped, the cabbages they grew. Now I see
their hands, the nails squared, earth biting down
in the furrows. I smell the stew of tobacco, hoe
handles and sweat, and today I long to go down
in a dense atmosphere of men working, the stone
that sinks below the lilies floating on water.

JIM MORRISON

Erotic comet, you ascended
into the hands of the Dismemberer,
whose eyes widened in fear
as he tore your used-up body.

At twenty, I was a foot soldier
in the children's army you rallied
under the orgiastic tent of your voice,
that promised in American winter
a festival of thaw, but hid
beneath its sullen shadow
an inward-growing rim of ice.

I have seen the photographs
of your grave at Pére-Lachaise,
to this day showered with roses
by others aspiring to your flight,
the Icaruses, the early-burning,
the moths hurled at the candle.

I was never one of those.
Yet last night while the radio
played "Waiting for the Sun,"
I saw your old aura draw itself
up again, of phoenix feathers
and snakeskin, and surprised myself
how badly I still wanted
to stand within your power.

WINTER SOLSTICE: IN THE SHADOW OF SATURN

1.

The outer planets roll distant in their orbits.
Vast arms, metallic and dense,
pull us into their cold mansion.

2.

We are condemned to live anonymously,
a blind burr grasping with tiny hooks the passing fur.

3.

Frustrated, heavy and gummy, the chest clogs
as if it were an automobile engine,
the oil not changed for a year.

4.

The leaden tolling we hear is our own
northern heart.

5.

Though we seem to move slowly, or not at all,
we are sailing in the shadow of Saturn,
in green poison without friction or sound.

THREE POEMS OF THE GULF WAR

AT THE START OF THE GULF WAR

At the corner convenience store, I write a check and can't find the date. Even the month has vanished! It has to do with the way the war is being reported—the bomb cargoes gone and "assets" in their place, the civilian casualties "collateral damage"....

Has someone bombed our memory? This must be the Stone Age, and no one yet has thought of the names of the Roman gods, no one has thought of Rome. There is an empire far more ancient we are seeing now, empire of strewn boulders, of bones picked clean by leathery birds circling.

There is a sadness in the regressed streets, of words lost, things unable to speak or be spoken of. I carry the groceries and newspaper to my car; suddenly it resembles an altar of rocks used for human sacrifice. Sleet sifts before the snow-encrusted tires bearing down like mill wheels driven by some unstoppable force.

REJOICING OVER DEATH

"...and a rusty nail, sticking up somewhere out of a plank,
does nothing day and night but rejoice over death."
— Rilke, *Wartime Letters*

Somewhere a rusty nail rejoices over the bombings,
and over the lesser animal and plant deaths.
Somewhere a rose of rust luxuriates in the vapor
of self-immolation it radiates in air,
in the sunset of metals where the torn missile
casings, exploded in the maternity hospital, fly.

Somewhere in unconcealed satisfaction
in a barn left to neglect in Connecticut or Kansas,
the last grain of wheat pilfered by rats,
the nail catches sunlight on bare floorboards
like the dried blood on the fingertip
of the princess who has sunk into sleep.

How many times this nail has rejoiced
in the hard choices so generous to death,
generous in grief, between the air war or ground war,
between killing the enemy or one's own,
the nail with its thin face gloating in the bunker,
leaning from the pale collar of the Commander-in-Chief.

CONTEMPT

We don't understand our grandparents'
satisfaction in not being famous—the hours spent
practicing the piano because one longed
to hear Chopin, the prairie light so calm
on weathered boards of the shed.

The scripture pages the old ones ponder
as death approaches are a walled garden
no longer noticed by the television watchers
admiring ingenious explosions
in the dawn sky over Mesopotamia.

What does it mean that we are bombing
the Garden? Contempt for simple
aspirations, for ordinary and peaceful
needs, shrieking down from dark cockpits
as the passive nation looks on.

Unable to play an instrument or dance,
we bomb the Baghdad of our human joy.
In the four-gated city, our grandfathers
and grandmothers become the children
Christ asked to "come unto Him."

A YOUNG MAN

Something in him wants to burst, confused,
not knowing whether it is a tree flowering
or an explosion, bearing heavy blossoms
or jagged metal fists. The snows
lie deep on his inheritance, the country
of wheat plowed under.

So much grief in his nervous laughter,
the smoky line of a shadow on the snow.
It is still alive in him, the strong root
ancient before the profit motive was invented,
the male root, black and melancholy, that grasps
the world and takes no more than it gives.

How does it profit a young man to plow an old
man under? He wanders in the snowy vineyard
where the scion hangs crucified on its trellis,
a bare forked branch under the winter sky,
the fruit asleep inside the wood,
in the ringed harbors without celebration.

ICE FISHING SHACKS ON GLEN LAKE

A half dozen shacks make a tiny village
on ice; they have a patched together look,
galvanized stovepipes rising from roofs,
plastic windows secured with strips of lath.
In this north country, people are rough-hewn—
both men and women walk with a bear-like gait.
A few men sit on sturdy orange buckets
outside the shacks, fathers fishing with sons.

My wife and I watch from our car
parked above the landing. The January sun
is generous, but there are things it can't give us.
Men and women can be generous with one another,
but what no woman can give me I feel
out there among the ice fishing shacks, what
my father would have given if he'd been able.

Last night, speaking with him long distance,
I sensed his loneliness trapped in the kitchen shadows.
Later, I dreamt of travelling with a teacher:
I would be given a test my father had failed.
I encountered a woman who had been changed into a sword,
a terrifying smile painted on her flat metal face.
She wore a kitchen apron and offered me freshly baked pie.
A voice warned, "This is the first obstacle!"

Where was the voice when my father needed to hear it?
Where was my father when the voice spoke?
I am in the middle of my life—I too
have become a sword, my steel untempered, brittle,
have learned to cut where the cord is weakest,
sever knots, and thrust myself away.

THE MUSKIE

In our parents' yard, a twenty-three pound
muskie's silver body hangs from your stringer.
You have me touch the pumice-like ridge
above the gills. The white throat gapes,
swallows imagination, like a man's tanned forearm,
to the elbow. I think of how a bullfrog
caught by the hundreds of back-curving needles
on the roof of the mouth would bleed and struggle
inside that cartilaginous case.

Your smile stiffens for the camera.
You became the fisherman
our father wanted one of his sons to be.
Those hours with him, too solitary,
out on the iron blue of the Chippewa
barbed into you while I escaped.
Today you're that fish, both predator and prey,
whose tigered back slides ferally and soundlessly
among the shifting shadows of its world.

Was it something of his frightened cruelty
you'd glimpsed turning in your own current
that July morning I drove up
and found you cloudstruck among the raspberries?
The channel is fast-moving and deep.
Only bubbles escape the terrible garden
breathing at the back of the jaws....
In you I see those rows of cat-like teeth hooked downward
and a drunken fisherman trailing his hand in the water.

"MY FATHER PROMISED ME A SWORD"

1.

The northern forest strides to the edge of the sea-cliff.
At dusk birds tell the story in darkening boughs:
The fortunate son has ridden for days to find
the rock where his father left a sword. It flashes
in sunset—the boy knows in his veins and sinews
the hilt will fit perfectly his hands. Red waves
recall the blaze of that great forge where old gods
are smelted down and new ones raised. The boy steps
to the edge of the cliff and easily draws the blade.

2.

A father can pass the sword willingly to his son,
bless the sunset waters with the glow of his leaving.
Or he can wield the sword until the end,
slash the sky in fury, scorch in afternoon,
rage his family to a desert. My father did neither.
I became an ordinary criminal and stole the sword.
In my new life as a thief, I rode the first horse
I could find—a crippled one—to encounter a dragon
who told me how, for money, he had killed his brother.

IV.
LIVING AS A CORMORANT

APPRENTICESHIP
For Christian Davis

1.

Let me return again to a day in my early thirties,
to the stout sun of July on leafy thistles
outside a one-room schoolhouse in Wisconsin.

Let me stand again before the unfinished door
arranging in my mind my lack of achievements
and my sudden reckless will to begin.

Give me back the flavor of that youthful
diffidence that held my reins overlong
but on whose back roads I discovered many

overlooked and neglected places. And finally
give me the salt taste of that fearfulness
with which I asked for what I wanted.

2.

At the door a man met me. His beard
was a thicket where I could hear
singing that held back the early frost.

Then something pushed me, a log into flames,
and I stepped forward in a story becoming
no one else's. That winter I undertook

the slow apprenticeships of words and wood,
diving among the fiery images, carrying ashes
from the grate of an old potbellied stove.

Across the fields of Ellsworth, days flared
through windows cloudy as isinglass, and burned.
Sometimes a poem showed me how to feed their heat.

HIGH PASTURE

In January, fearful that the fabric
is becoming ugly and cheap, and that the generosity
of the teachers, unwanted, may turn and walk
away, I climb the snowed-in tractor road
from the barn to the high pasture.

Among iced furrows I look for a dull
shine in the year's beginning.
Stubble of autumn's harvest stitches
the white cap of the hill, an ochre, long-lined
poem the crow's tongue stutters toward.

Cornshucks flag barbed wire in the wind.
Binders and spreaders—occult apparatus
of a greener season—hunker in brooding.
Their forks and disks attend downward
a slowly pooling spring beneath the snow.

Old fields wait patiently for the new growth
that is their hope. The young are beautiful,
but the master weaver, wizening over his skeins,
sends cranes soaring on the sky of his loom.
For human beings, it is more important to create

beauty than embody it. The river parted
by immense boulders, the house folded among black trees,
songs sung by a man and woman in the house on New Year's Day—
what are these but a fabric to clothe
our swiftly traveling senses in this world?

New Year's Day, 1990

THE WATER TANK

Walking near the barbed wire fences of the cemetery, I notice wild roses twining on the strands. Their watery pink petals have wilted in the midday heat. Green flames of corn on hillsides reach toward the June sun.

I cut half a dozen of the rose stems with a pocketknife. By a southward-facing row of pines, I find pump water in a galvanized stock tank. Sun and pine shade dapple the dusty rim. The water does not offer coolness: Film lies on the surface; two plastic milk jugs drift, half-sunk; a scrap of tinfoil crumples the light. I bend to dip the roses' stems in the luke-warm water with its wrinkled skin of dust.

What at first I took for a layer of black silt across the bottom turns out to be a bed of mosquito larvae. Seen up close, the whole mass wriggles like a thousand-fingered black rubber glove. Each larva body bends like a pulled bow, then jerks taut to move a little farther in the water.

So many we've loved have already vanished where these tiny archers aim in feebleness and squalor, into the horizon between the two dates carved on stone! On one of the grave-stones, a large hand receiving a small hand expresses confidence in an old promise.

THE ART OF THE POETRY READING

LISTENING TO ROBERT BLY AT UNITY CHURCH

Why don't our heads flop to one side,
pulled down by a grief in earth
that fuses boulders to its titanic ribs?
In this light sanctuary, we must resist
being lifted too readily—there is labor hidden
in these stanzas born effortlessly as we hear them.
The poet has piled the stones of his life
year after year on the unpromising pastures.

Isn't the real work done with a purpose not our own?
I look down, see wrists enter white cuffs
and black coatsleeves as my grandfather's did.
Behind a wedding ring stands some gold
my eyes have not seen. Childhood has gone inside
mute things. My hands do not belong to me
but to someone who has worn and discarded
generations of hands in my family.

THOMAS McGRATH READING

Ever the old pirate with his patched eye, he mocks
gently mortality's remainders. Speaking lines on the 60s—
"so many young men with long hair, so many poets with short
Breath"—the voice falls off in witty self-recognition.

Taking up between stanzas the cigarette he won't let die,
fiercely, in a hand gloved as if against the page's fire,
he recites for the instant commune of the young. His feet
run swiftly, six to the line, without need of a cane.

He proves that the old maize of listening still knows
how to leaf from American deafness: Even those in
front-row seats lean hard to distinguish tropes
faint but pungent, elaborately braided as ropes of garlic.

From long use, the voice's weakness has become in itself
noble, the longshoreman's moon off the end of the wharf,
dismembered by the sea and rushing each moment toward
a union it has imagined but cannot now achieve.

Hungry Mind Bookstore, St. Paul, January 18, 1989

THE PLOWSHARE

Gaubert the blacksmith had promised me,
"You shall have your plow." But how would they
work their marriage of fire and metal now, those
hands left to perch on the polished head of a cane?

Still I agreed to sweep beneath his narrow cot
and struck the share wrapped in burlap,
his last. With thick, astonished fingers
I dragged it out and bared its steel

managing to trap and stir more light
than I'd guessed the dim bedroom of an old
man's dying could hold. Radiant and grave,
it led the entire lineage of plows.

Pride gripped the slackened body:
I watched old Gaubert's thin neck quiver,
his hands clench fiercely the cane.
At that instant the forge he'd left cold

on the mountain must surely have glowed!
And tears of spring rain poured into
that brightness I'd scooped in my arms,
careless of its heft, and held against

my chest as if it were a son,
opener of earth and life,
its millboard swollen with the myriad
wheat souls swarming toward birth.

After a scene in Pagnol's film Harvest

THE POEM ASLEEP IN THE HEART

Stiff grasses, long-leggéd and bare,
quiver by the frozen lakeside
where the March snow has turned back.

To their caps of seed that shake
thin rattles in the wind
we bring care for the dead of our own tribe.

But some sprightliness persists in these
despite their frailty—young gold
leaps the whole length of their hollow stems,

journeys with them into the under-
world where their lives are bundled
and stored in the sheaf of their time.

As generations of mountain farmers
build terraces, men and women
carrying each stone to a place

intended for it, unseen hands
fit our lives to the lives before us.
So the old dead men and women in us

join to the life we give outward.
It is the life already lived that calls
to the new life, the poem already written

that calls to the poem asleep in the heart.

WEEK ALONE IN A CABIN

Autumn burns off vanity, leaves a reticent
beauty in crystal grasses that tremble
at the shins of the scrub apple tree.

October winds jostle the cabin. With the world's
steel tightened around me, how the simplest
emotions wounded my chest! I longed

for the open pasture on a spotted birch leaf.
When I could walk its serrated road away
from the city, I found a rhythm for love.

For days I've chewed on the old, accustomed
pain of being bound—suddenly, as if I'd
gnawed the twine restraining one of those

weathered rounds of hay that kneel like sleeping
bison at the edge of these wooded fields,
I've broken through to an abundance.

Finding you again at every turn I've taken
around this shack pitched on its knoll, I've drunk
deeply of the generous, free way things in solitude,

clarified by a silence that makes room for them,
pour from the buckets of their names—*chair,*
window, apple, pump, frost, star—a sweet water.

SPIRAL WEEDS UNDER THE WATER

Off the end of this abandoned dock
fallen birch trunks roll in mire,
their bark, once blindingly white,
discolored by mud and algae. So it's
true that the father-eagle
of this world, plummeted from
his high vantage, will not fly again.

Then what is left for us now,
sitting while the light of day,
its work nearly finished, walks
away from us across the water
on thinning rays? I look down,
notice growing on the bottom sun-
lit weeds that spiral tightly.

Their ends, parted like small mouths
or the lips of the phallos,
breathe below the surface,
roots planted among the feathery
muck and disjoined halves of shells
which life has left behind.
But must our imagination follow

the path the world is taking?
Here and there in the stagnant
shallows a glowing weed veers
from its carefully wound course
and streams upward with muscular
serpent motions as if escaping
toward the breaking gold.

DREAM OF AN INHERITANCE

In the dream I balanced high
on a wobbly tower of crates
stacked in an open truck.
A man with a red beard handed me

a crate containing my inheritance.
Inside were vegetables from my
father's garden: long shanks of celery,
brooding foreheads of tomatoes.

I closed the box, tucked it under
my arm to clamber earthward,
but the sideboards of the truck
I stepped down on for a ladder

swung outward. I lost footing,
began to fall, then looked down
and saw my father's face. He hugged
the boards, reached upward

to guide the loose rails where my feet
needed to meet them. In my body
I could feel the fathers before him
reaching through his body. One-handed,

right arm still firm around the crate,
I swung easily, almost ape-like,
the rest of the way down.
On the ground was a firepit for cooking.

CORMORANT

Buoyant on the chill harbor,
I would live then as a cormorant,

my oily feathers cutting the waves.
I would turn my seeing downward,

reach after only the deepest prey,
and surrender to my unyielding master

without complaint the silver and
elusive catch of each descent.

Around my neck some cunning
surpassing my own had sealed

a ring to force upward my gleaning
of the secretive schools below,

food for someone I'd never seen.
At day's end a few fish left

in the buckets were mine to keep,
enough though neither large nor many.

ABOUT THE AUTHOR

Thomas R. Smith was born in 1948 and grew up in Cornell, Wisconsin, a paper mill town on the banks of the Chippewa River. He majored in English at the University of Wisconsin - River Falls, coming to poetry through his teachers there. In the late 70s, inspired by the work of Rimbaud and Baudelaire during a year's travel in Europe, he turned his energies toward the prose poem, a form he now finds uniquely suited to expressing a spiritual response to landscape.

In the early 80s, Smith directed Artspeople, a rural-based arts organization serving farm communities in western Wisconsin. A poet, essayist and editor, his work has appeared in numerous journals in the U.S., Canada, and abroad. His poems were included in *Editor's Choice II* (The Spirit That Moves Us Press), a gathering of the best of the American small press. His first book of poetry, *Keeping the Star* was published in 1988 by New Rivers Press. He edited *Walking Swiftly: Writings and Images on the Occasion of Robert Bly's 65th Birthday* (Ally Press, 1992; HarperCollins, 1993) and *What Happened When He Went to the Store for Bread* (Nineties Press, 1993), a selection of the late Canadian poet Alden Nowlan, whose poems he encountered while traveling in the Maritimes in 1989. Around the same time he became a founding editor of *Inroads*, a journal on men and soul. Smith views his work in the spirit of the French poet Ponge's statement that artists "have to open a workshop and take the world in for repairs." He lives with his wife, the artist Krista Spieler, in Minneapolis.

ABOUT THE ARTIST

Fine artist Perry L. Ingli, a native of Wisconsin, lives and works out of his Minneapolis studio, from which he travels to experience and create his synthesis of the landscapes and waterways of the region. His artworks have recently been acquired for the collections of the Minnesota Historical Society and the Science Museum of Minnesota, as well as by many private collectors. He began his sumac series (of which the cover drawing of this book is an example) in 1987 in locations in Wisconsin and Minnesota. He is currently working on large-scale panoramas of Lake Pepin and the Apostle Islands and studying conversational Japanese with an eye toward a studio sabbatical in Japan. He is represented by the Suzanne Kohn Gallery in Saint Paul, Minnesota.